A JOURNEY WITH JONAH
A Man on the Run

WAYNE DUNAWAY

A JOURNEY WITH JONAH
A Man on the Run
Revised Edition

Copyright © 2017 Wayne Dunaway

All Rights Reserved. No part of this book may be reproduced or transmitted in any form or by any means without written permission from the author except for the inclusion of quotations in a review.

Printed in the United States of America
ISBN 978-0-9993796-1-5

Unless otherwise noted all Scripture quotations are taken from the New King James Version, NKJV®. Copyright © 1982 by Thomas Nelson. Used by permission. All rights reserved.

Other Translations:
The Holy Bible, English Standard Version. ESV® Permanent Text Edition® (2016). Copyright © 2001 by Crossway Bibles, a publishing ministry of Good News Publishers.

Holy Bible, New International Version®, NIV® Copyright ©1973, 1978, 1984, 2011 by Biblica, Inc.® Used by permission. All rights reserved worldwide.

Holy Bible, New Living Translation, copyright © 1996, 2004, 2015 by Tyndale House Foundation. Used by permission of Tyndale House Publishers Inc., Carol Stream, Illinois 60188. All rights reserved.

King James Version (KJV)   Public Domain
American Standard Version (ASV) Public Domain

DEDICATION

To my wife Pat, my daughter Tawana, and my son Bryan, a Christian family that would make any man proud. NOTE: Even though it has now been over fifteen years since this statement was first made it is still very true. A lot of things have changed during those years but being proud of these three is not one of them.

TABLE OF CONTENTS

PREFACE   7
POEM: THE STORY OF JONAH   9
INTRODUCTION   11

CHAPTER ONE   16
Chapter Outline
Lesson 1
Scripture: Jonah 1:1-3
The Fleeing
Lesson 2
Scripture: Jonah 1:4-16
The Fear
Lesson 3
Scripture: Jonah 1:17
The Fish

CHAPTER TWO   44
Chapter Outline
Lesson 4
Scripture: Jonah 2:1-3
The Venture
Lesson 5
Scripture: Jonah 2:4-9
The Vow
Lesson 6
Scripture: Jonah 2:10
The Vomit

CHAPTER THREE 72
Chapter Outline
Lesson 7
Scripture: Jonah 3:1-4
The Message
Lesson 8
Scripture: Jonah 3:5-9
The Mourning
Lesson 9
Scripture: Jonah 3:10
The Mercy

CHAPTER FOUR 99
Chapter Outline
Lesson 10
Scripture: Jonah 4:1-11
Jonah Resenting

PREFACE

A JOURNEY WITH JONAH **DEALS WITH** a man on the run. Jonah runs *from* God in chapter one, *to* God in chapter two, *with* God in chapter three, and *against* God in chapter four. He is a son on the run who has very little fun.

The book of Jonah is, in reality, a book that deals with attitude adjustments. The people of Nineveh needed an attitude adjustment when it came to sin; Jonah needed an attitude adjustment when it came to souls. Both needed to learn to bow to the will of God and both got what they needed.

A Journey with Jonah will be a profitable study for anyone who will take the lessons to heart. All of us at times need adjustments in our attitudes regarding God, His word, our responsibility to others, and a host of other areas covered in this book. Hopefully, God can use these truths to help us make whatever adjustments we need to make in living the Christian life. God's *truth* can *build* character while God's *testing* can *reveal* character. And God can use both to help us be what we need to be.

One thing that can help us realize what adjustments need to be made in our own lives, and to then make them, is the study of the book of Jonah. It's a whale of a tale that can help us to do well, especially when we fail. And since we all fail at times, we all need to learn from Jonah to face our failures with faith. We also need to learn from the Ninevites that we can all change, no matter how bad we are or how long we have been bad, if we will respond positively to God and His word.

It is my hope that you will study *A Journey with Jonah,* realizing that there are attitude adjustments that the Lord needs to make in all of us at times. If these lessons help you in any way to make those adjustments and become a better Christian, then the time and effort spent in making this book available will have surely been worthwhile. Blessings!

Wayne Dunaway

Revised Edition
October, 2017

THE STORY OF JONAH

Chapter One:
Nineveh's wicked so Jonah must preach,
But he tries to flee from the Lord's mighty reach.
Then he receives the reward for his wish,
Three days and nights inside a great fish.

Chapter Two:
But Jonah repents while down in the fish,
And sees how completely absurd was his wish.
He promises now to obey God's command,
And promptly is vomited out on the land.

Chapter Three:
Jonah's now preaching and Nineveh hears,
And they go in sackcloth because of their fears.
They fast and they pray that God may be stirred,
They are rewarded because His wrath is deferred.

Chapter Four:
Jonah gets mad when God freely spares,
And he watches the city to see how it fares.
God sends a plant as well as a worm,
Jonah gets angry and his lesson he learns.
(Unknown author/revised).

INTRODUCTION

I. THE PRINCIPLE CHARACTER.

THE MAIN CHARACTER OF OUR study is the prophet Jonah who was commissioned to go to Nineveh to preach. He is first mentioned in the Bible in 2 Kings 14:25. He was the son of Amittai (1:1). The Lord Himself verified that Jonah was a historical character (Matt. 12:39-41). From the accounts given of him we learn that he was a:

Religious Person.
He is called the Lord's servant (2 Kings 14:25). He admitted that he feared the Lord (1:9). He prayed unto the Lord his God (2:1; 2:6).

Reliable Prophet.
The land restored to Israel during the reign of Jeroboam II was "according to the word of the Lord God of Israel, which He had spoken through His servant Jonah" (2 Kings 14:25). Therefore, Jonah was a true prophet of God. (See Deuteronomy 18:21-22.)

Relentless Patriot.
He was a pitiless, persistent person who loved and loyally supported his country. It was probably his love for his country that caused him to want the Ninevites destroyed.

Reluctant Preacher.
In the book of Jonah we find Jonah unwilling to do what God commissioned him to do.

II. THE PROBLEM CONFRONTED.

The problem that God deals with in Jonah is twofold:
A. The Sinful City.
B. The Lack of Pity.

III. THE POINT COVERED.

The main point covered (or theme of the book) is that God is a gracious God, merciful, slow to anger, and very kind (4:2). God loves the whole world and, because of that, He is gracious to:
A. The Reluctant Preacher (chs. 1-2).
B. The Rebellious People (ch. 3).
C. The Racially Prejudiced (ch. 4).

IV. THE PROPHET'S CONDUCT.

One good way of looking at the four chapters of the book is to notice Jonah's conduct in each chapter. For example, we have:

A. Jonah Rebelling (ch. l).
B. Jonah Repenting (ch. 2).
C. Jonah Responding (ch. 3).
D. Jonah Resenting (ch. 4).

V. THE PREDOMINANT CHARACTERISTICS.

The most noticeable traits of God we see in the book of Jonah are:
A. God's Displeasure with Sin (ch. 1:2-4, 13).
B. God's Discipline of Saints (ch. l).
C. God's Desire to Save (chs. 1-4).

DISCUSSION QUESTIONS

PRELIMINARY

1. How do we know Jonah was a true prophet?

2. What is the main lesson taught in the book of Jonah?

3. What is remembered most about the book of Jonah?
    a. What great truths, other than the one remembered most, are presented in the book?
    b. Discuss our nature of emphasizing the sensational at the expense of other great truths.

4. What did Jonah have in common with the Jews of Jesus' day? (See Luke 9:51-56.)

5. How would most people today like to treat their enemies? What does Jesus teach us to do regarding our enemies? (See Matthew 5:44; Romans 12:20-21.)

6. Was Jonah's prejudice against Nineveh based on race or religion or both? Discuss the problem of racial and religious prejudice in today's world.

7. Is there anything wrong with loving and supporting one's country and government? Explain your answer. (See Romans 13:1-7; 1 Timothy 2:1-4; 1 Peter 2:13-15.)

8. Discuss the predominant characteristics of God as seen in the book of Jonah.

9. Which characteristic of God stands out most in your mind as you think about the book of Jonah?

10. What did Jesus say about the preaching of Jonah?

CHAPTER ONE

JONAH REBELLING
(Running from God)

I. THE FLEEING (1:1-3). The fleeing is dared.

A. The Revelation: His duty was clear (1:1-2).
 1. The word (v.1).
 2. The warning (v.2a).
 3. The wickedness (v.2b).

B. The Refusal: He refuses to hear (1:3).
 1. Where he fled (v.3a).
 2. What he found (v.3b).
 3. Who paid the fare (v.3c).

II. THE FEAR (1:4-16). The fear is shared.

A. The Explanation for the Fear (1:4-10).
 1. The reason for it (v.4).
  a. The present danger from the storm (v.4a).
  b. The possible damage to the ship (v.4b).
 2. The reaction to it (v.5).

a. They cry to their gods (v.5c).
  b. They cast out their goods (v.5b).
 3. The realization from it (vv.6-10).
  a. What the mariners decided (vv.6-7a).
  b. What the mariners discovered (v.7b).
  c. What the mariners demanded (vv.8-10).

 B. The Elimination of the Fear (1:11-16).
  1. The request of the mariners (vv.11- 12).
   a. The question was concise (v.11).
   b. The answer was courageous (v.12).
  2. The reluctance of the mariners (vv.13-14).
   a. The attempt for the land (v.13).
   b. The appeal to the Lord (v.14).
  3. The reverence of the mariners (vv.15-16).
   a. Seen in their submission (v.15).
   b. Seen in their sacrifice (v.16a).
   c. Seen in their statements (v.16b).

III. THE FISH (1:17). The fish is prepared.

A. The Preparation of the Fish (v.17).
 1. The miracle recorded.
 2. The motive revealed.

B. The Preservation in the Fish (v.17b).
 1. The place where he was contained.
 2. The period in which he remained.

LESSON 1

SCRIPTURE READING
(Jonah 1:1-3)

N OW THE WORD OF THE *Lord came to Jonah the son of Amittai, saying, 2"Arise, go to Nineveh, that great city, and cry out against it; for their wickedness has come up before Me." 3 But Jonah arose to flee to Tarshish from the presence of the Lord. He went down to Joppa, and found a ship going to Tarshish; so he paid the fare, and went down into it, to go with them to Tarshish from the presence of the Lord. (NKJV)*

LESSON 1

THE FLEEING
(The fleeing is dared)
Jonah 1:1-3

IN THIS FIRST CHAPTER, WE see Jonah fleeing. It was the *fleeing* in verses 1-3, that led to the *fear* in verses 4-16, that led to the *fish* in verse 17. We will observe two things in these first three verses, namely the revelation to Jonah and the refusal of Jonah.

THE REVELATION TO JONAH.

The revelation was clear (1:1-2). Jonah could not have misunderstood his duty: "Arise, go to Nineveh . . . and cry against it." The duty of every man is to "fear God and keep his commandments" (Eccl. 12:13). Like Jonah, we all have a duty to God and that duty, of necessity, must be clear (Eph. 3:4; 5:17). There are some things that are hard to be understood (2 Pet. 3:15-16), but duty to God is not one of them. Those things that we must believe and do in order to get right and stay right are clearly revealed to us just as Jonah's duty was to him.

As we think about the revelation to Jonah, let's notice what these two verses say about the *word* (1:1). The word evidently came directly to Jonah. Today God speaks to us through His Son (Heb. 1:1-2). The Son speaks to us through His word and His Spirit (Jn. 12:48; Jam. 1:25; Rom. 8:14.). That is the reason we need seek (Isa. 34:16), search (Jn. 5:39), and study (2 Tim. 2:15) to find His will for our lives. God speaks to us today just as surely as He spoke to Jonah, but: *Today if we hear the voice of the Rock of Ages, someone's going to have to turn the pages.* The word that came to Jonah was a *warning* (1:2a). It was a warning to Nineveh. He was to "cry out against it." He warned them that Nineveh "shall be overthrown." Noah was "warned of God of things not seen as yet" (Heb. 11:7). Paul "... ceased not to warn every one night and day with tears ..." (Acts 20:31). (See also 1 Corinthians 4:14.) An important part of preaching Christ involves "warning every man, and teaching every man in all wisdom..." (Col. 1:28). There are times today when God expects us to "cry against" certain things. We can't always be mild-mannered teachers who teach mild-mannered lessons to mild-mannered people on how to be more mild mannered. Sometimes we must reprove and rebuke as well as exhort (2 Tim. 4:1-3). Jonah warned them concerning their *wickedness* (1:2b). In the revelation to Jonah, the *word* was a *warning* about the *wickedness*. The wickedness of the Ninevites had come up before God, and He was about to bring judgment on them because of it. In a very real sense, God knows about all wickedness and sin (Prov. 15:3; Heb. 4:13). And sooner or later, it will come up before Him to be dealt with. God even knows the hearts of all men (Acts 1:24; 1 Sam. 16:7; Mk. 16:14). He knows about the thoughts and imaginations of the heart and whether or not they are evil (Gen. 6:5; Matt. 9:4). Therefore, God knows not only who is wicked, but also who would be wicked if they could get away with it. One (unknown) poet spoke well when he said:

You may fool the hapless public,
You may fool ole Tim and Tod,
You may fool most everybody,
But you can't fool God.

THE REFUSAL OF JONAH.

Jonah's *duty was clear*, but he *refused to hear*. God had said to "arise and go," but Jonah decided to tell Him "No!" Like many today, he rebelled against what God had revealed. Notice in verse three where he *fled* (1:3a). The text says he "rose up to flee to Tarshish." In ancient times, Tarshish was likely a prominent city. Though its exact location has not been determined, many scholars believe it to have been on the southwestern coast of Spain. That was quite a distance from Joppa! But without regard to location, Tarshish has come to represent running away from duty. Instead of doing what God had said, Jonah rose up and away he fled—toward Tarshish! Any time we run away from our duty to God, we are headed for our Tarshish. Note also that he rose up to flee to Tarshish "from the presence of the Lord." Jonah should have known what David had already written about fleeing from the Lord's presence (Ps. 139:7-12). Because no matter how hard or how far we run, that is something that cannot be done. Yet many today, even some members of the church, seem to think we can get away from the presence of the Lord. We too, flee to get into things we shouldn't do, or run away from things that we should do. But, like Jonah, we never succeed (Prov. 15:3; Heb. 4:13). Notice also what he *found* (1:3b). The verse says, "He found a ship." Isn't that convenient? He was trying to flee from his duty and Satan had the boat ready. Of course, anytime we want to run from our duty, Satan will have the boat ready. For example, sinners all have a duty to God. They *must* obey the gospel (believe in Jesus) to be saved (Heb. 5:8-9). But anytime they are ready to run from that duty, Satan will have them a boat full of excuses for not obeying: "I'm afraid I can't hold out;" or "There are too many hypocrites in the church;" or perhaps, "I need to get some things straightened out first." Just as in the case of Jonah, Satan has the boat ready if we decide to run. Christians, too, have a duty to the Lord to go teach as they have ability and opportunity (Matt. 28:19; Mk. 16:15). But if we decide to run from duty like Jonah did, Satan will have the boat ready: "I don't know enough about the Bible;" or "I just can't talk to people;" or "I'm afraid I'll offend someone." But the ready way is not always the right way. The convenient way is not always the Christian way. If we always follow the path of least resistance, it will surely lead to trouble: *Follow the path of least resistance, that's what the rivers do. 'Course that's what makes them crooked, and it will do the same for you.*

Notice not only where he fled and what he found, but note also *who paid the fare.* The text says: "He paid the fare" (1:3a). Of course, that shouldn't surprise us, because any time we flee from our duty to God, it's going to cost us. Be sure your sin will find you out (Num. 32:23). Be not deceived, whatsoever a man sows, that shall he also reap (Gal. 6:7). Observe also that the text says that he went *down* to Joppa and *down* into the ship. When we are fleeing from our duty to God, the only way to go is down.

In this first chapter, Jonah is *rebelling.* In these first three verses we have studied about his *fleeing* as we looked at the revelation to Jonah and the refusal of Jonah. His *fleeing* brought about a storm which brought about some *fear* in the mariners on the ship. The *fleeing* in verses 1-3 led to the *fear* in verses 4-16 which will be the subject of our next study.

DISCUSSION QUESTIONS

LESSON 1

1. Discuss the statement: Duty, of necessity, must be clear.

2. Explain how God speaks to us today.

3. Discuss some of the warnings that are found in the New Testament.

4. Why did God intend to destroy Nineveh?

5. Since the exact location of the ancient city of Tarshish has not been determined, explain how one might "flee to Tarshish" today.

6. Discuss some Bible passages that deal with God's omnipresence.

7. Using Jonah to illustrate the point, explain why the convenient way is not always the right way.

8. What are some of the excuses men use today for not obeying the gospel (believing in Jesus)?

9. What are some of the excuses Christians use for failing to carry out the Great Commission?

10. What proof do we have that sin will cost us?

LESSON 2

SCRIPTURE READING
(Jonah 1:4-16)

BUT THE LORD SENT OUT *a great wind on the sea, and there was a mighty tempest on the sea, so that the ship was about to be broken up. 5 Then the mariners were afraid; and every man cried out to his god, and threw the cargo that was in the ship into the sea, to lighten the load. But Jonah had gone down into the lowest parts of the ship, had lain down, and was fast asleep. 6 So the captain came to him, and said to him, "What do you mean, sleeper? Arise, call on your God; perhaps your God will consider us, so that we may not perish." 7 And they said to one another, "Come, let us cast lots, that we may know for whose cause this trouble has come upon us." So they cast lots, and the lot fell on Jonah. 8 Then they said to him, "Please tell us! For whose cause is this trouble upon us? What is your occupation? And where do you come from? What is your country? And of what people are you?" 9 So he said to them, "I am a Hebrew; and I fear the Lord, the God of heaven, who made the sea and the dry land." 10 Then the men were* *exceedingly afraid, and said to him, "Why have you done this?" For the men knew that he fled from the presence of the Lord, because he had told them. 11 Then they said to him, "What shall we do to you that the sea may be calm for us?"—for the sea was growing more tempestuous. 12 And he said to them, "Pick me up and throw me into the sea; then the sea will become calm for you. For I know that this great tempest is because of me." 13 Nevertheless the men rowed hard to return to land, but they could not, for the sea continued to grow more tempestuous against them. 14 Therefore they cried out to the Lord and said, "We pray, O Lord, please do not let us perish for this man's life, and do not charge us with innocent blood; for You, O Lord, have done as it pleased You." 15 So they picked up Jonah and threw him into the sea, and the sea ceased from its raging. 16 Then the men feared the Lord exceedingly, and offered a sacrifice to the Lord and took vows. (NKJV)*

LESSON 2

THE FEAR
(The fear is shared)
Jonah 1:4-16

IN THIS STUDY WE WILL concentrate on the fear that was shared by the mariners. After the fleeing was dared by the missionary, the fear was shared by the mariners. We will observe the explanation for the fear and the elimination of the fear.

THE EXPLANATION FOR THE FEAR (1:4-10).

First, we have the *reason* for it (1:4). One reason for the fear among the mariners was the *present danger from the storm* (1:4a). The verse says the Lord sent out a great wind and there was a mighty storm in the sea. Another reason for the fear was the *possible damage to the ship* (v.1:4b). The ship was likely to be broken up. Of course, anytime a child of God flees from his duty to God the storm is coming. The Bible clearly teaches that God disciplines/trains those He loves and chastens every child He receives (Heb.

12:5-12; Rev. 3:19). There may be suffering without sinning, but there can be no sinning without suffering. And sometimes one may suffer because of the sin of someone else as was the case here, when the mariners suffered from the storm because of the sin of Jonah (1:12b). Next notice the *reaction* to it (1:5). The sailors were afraid and they began to cry to their gods (1:5a). They also cast out their goods (1:5b). And while their prayer wouldn't do any good because it was addressed to false gods, they did have the right idea about it. Observe that the mariners *cried* and *cast*. They didn't just cry. They didn't just cast. They both cried *and* cast. Christians today need to learn what the heathen sailors knew about prayer. They knew that *crying* wouldn't do any good without *casting*. That is, praying wouldn't do any good without working. We need to be constantly reminded that along with praying there must be some obeying. If we are going to do the asking, we need also to do the seeking and knocking (Matt. 7:7-8). The passage in James 2:14-26 was written primarily to Christians to remind us that faith that works is faith that wins. We need to pray as if everything depended on God and work as if everything depended on us and then we can get things done.

Observe also that Jonah was fast asleep (1:5c). The only man on the whole ship who knew the true God was asleep! That is much like Christians today. Many others are going about teaching, studying, visiting newcomers, showing concern for those in need, and doing many other good works. And where are we? Asleep on the boat! If Jonah had continued sleeping, he would have gone down with the ship. And if we continue our sleeping, we could possibly go down with the world. Like the disciples of our Lord, we are asleep when we ought to be watching (Matt. 26:40). Again and again the New Testament tells Christians to awake out of sleep (Rom. 13:11; 1 Cor. 15:34; Eph. 5:14). We all must wake up and get up from our spiritual slumber if we expect to be blessed with that number. We may not lose our salvation, but we'll miss out on a lot of opportunities to help others know Jesus. We must wake up and get up, but never shut up, back up, give up, or let up until the church is built up and finally taken up. Now note the *realization* that came from the fear (1:6-10). The mariners finally realize that someone's wrong-doing has caused the danger and the captain rebukes Jonah for being a sleeper (1:6). But then I want us to notice *what the mariners decided* (1:7c). They decided to cast lots that they might "know for whose cause this evil is upon us" (1:7c). Notice next *what the mariners discovered.* They discovered that the prophet was the problem because the lot fell on Jonah. The statement in Proverbs 16:33 surely applies here: "The lot is cast into the lap, but its every decision is from the Lord." In other words, the Lord loaded the lots (2:3). Finally notice also *what the mariners demanded.* They demanded to know the facts about Jonah and he tells them that he was fleeing from the presence of the Lord who had made the sea and dry land.

THE ELIMINATION OF THE FEAR (1:11-16).

After looking at the explanation for the fear, we now need to see the elimination of the fear. But before the *elimination*, there was the *examination*. This is seen in the *request* of the mariners (1:11-12). The question to Jonah was *concise*. They asked him simply: "What shall we do to you that the sea may be calm to us?" (1:11). The answer of Jonah was *courageous*. He told them plainly: "Pick me up and throw me into the sea" (1:12). Most people would probably say: "You can turn me over your knee, but don't you throw me into that sea." But not so with Jonah—he courageously told them what had to happen. Proverbs 13:15 says the way of the transgressor is hard. But observe the *reluctance* of the mariners (1:13-14). Note how reluctant the mariners are. Instead of throwing out the man, they make an attempt for the land. The verse says, "the men rowed hard to return to land" (1:13a). Observe that God wanted Jonah in the water, but they wanted to keep him in the ship. But they couldn't keep him in the ship (1:13b). Why? Because God was about ready to sink that whole ship to get Jonah into the water. The passage says: "The sea continued to grow more tempestuous against them" (1:13c).

Today God casts certain people out of the ship or fellowship of the church. But many times some brethren will *row hard* to keep them in. We need to learn from Jonah chapter one that that kind of thing must not be done. We need to learn from this section of Jonah that God disciplines wayward disciples for our own good. See 1 Corinthians 5:1-13 and Revelation 3:19. It also needs to be emphasized that no one man ought to be allowed to sink a whole ship. Sometimes there is a present day "Diotrophes" who needs to be thrown overboard, so to speak, before he destroys a whole church (3 Jn. 1:9-10). There are some who are going to rule or ruin, boss or cost, and they don't care if all are lost. But it seems that John was going to visit the church and take care of Diotrophes (3 Jn. 1:10). And there are times when the church must do the same today. After failing in their *attempt for the land,* the mariners then made an *appeal to the Lord* (1:14). They asked that they be not held responsible for Jonah's life. It is amazing that these heathen sailors had more compassion on another human being than did a Hebrew servant of the true God.

We also see the *reverence* of the mariners (1:15-16). Their reverence is seen first in their *submission.* They cast Jonah into the sea (1:15). That was not easy. Nor do we always understand why God tells us to do certain things, but we need to know that the only way to have real peace is to follow God's instructions. It's only then that the sea will cease from her raging (1:15b). Their reverence is also seen in their *sacrifice.* They then offer a sacrifice to the Lord (1:16a). All true reverence for the Lord will manifest itself in submission and sacrifice. Their reverence is not only seen in their submission and sacrifice, but also in their *statements.* The text says they made vows (1:16 c). The New Testament teaches that we are to serve God today with reverence and godly fear (Heb. 12:28). This involves submission (Jam. 4:7), sacrifice (Rom. 12:1), and living up to our statements (Heb. 10:23). We end this section concerning the *fear* with Jonah in the sea. It was the *fleeing* in verses 1-3 that lead to the *fear* of verses 4-16, which leads to our final study in this first chapter concerning the *fish* in verse 17.

DISCUSSION QUESTIONS

LESSON 2

1. What proof is there in this first chapter that the innocent sometimes suffer because of the guilty? Discuss some of the ways this happens today.

2. What important lesson can we learn from the heathen mariners about prayer?

3. How can a present day Christian be "asleep in the ship"?

4. Give an example (other than the one in this lesson) where lots were cast to make a selection? (Hint: Acts 1).

5. What proof do we have that Jonah was a courageous person?

6. In Proverbs 13:15 what does God say about the way of the transgressor? How does Jonah illustrate this truth?

7. Explain how the mariners were involved in the discipline of Jonah and how God may use other believers to discipline/correct/train wayward members today?

8. In what way did the heathen sailors show more compassion than Jonah did? Discuss similar situations that occur today.

9. Discuss the reverence of the mariners as compared to the reverence expected of Christians today.

10. Explain why God disciplines His children.

LESSON 3

SCRIPTURE READING
(Jonah 1:17)

N**OW THE LORD HAD PREPARED** *a great fish to swallow up Jonah. And Jonah was in the belly of the fish three days and three nights. (KJV)*

LESSON 3

THE FISH
(The fish is prepared)
Jonah 1:17

IN THIS STUDY WE CONCENTRATE on the fish that was prepared by the Lord. The fear that was shared by the mariners caused them to throw Jonah overboard. And the fish that the Lord had to prepare was ready to take it from there. In this study we will observe the preparation of the fish and Jonah's preservation in the fish.

THE PREPARATION OF THE FISH (1:17a).

First, we have the *miracle recorded*. The text says: "Now the Lord had prepared a great fish..." This definitely involved the miraculous. The *fate was planned* and the *fish was prepared*. Both involved the omniscience and omnipotence of God. His supernatural knowledge and His supreme power are clearly seen in this event. There are some today who deny the miracles of the Old Testament yet claim to believe in Christ and the New Testament. Yet many of the things that they call into question are verified and supported in the New Testament. Think about a few of the following examples. The *creation* of man (Gen. 1-2). See Matthew 19:4-6; Mark 10:6. The *conversation* with the serpent (Gen. 3). See 2 Corinthians 11:3; 1 Timothy 2:13-14. The *translation* of Enoch (Gen. 5:24). See Hebrews 11:5. The *salvation* of Noah (Gen. 6-9). See Matthew 24:37-39. The *annihilation* of Sodom (Gen. 19). See Luke 17:28-29. The *communication* from the bush (Exod. 3). See Mark 12:26. The *education* of Pharaoh (Exod. 7-12). See Romans 9:17. The *liberation* of Israel (Exod. 14:13-30). See 1 Corinthians 10:1-2; Hebrews 11:29. The *elimination* of Naaman's leprosy (2 Kings 5). See Luke 4:27. The *preparation* of the fish (1:.17). See Matthew 12:39-41. Besides the preparation of the great fish, there are also other events in the book of Jonah that show God's supernatural power and control. For example: a. "But the Lord sent out a great wind ..." (1:4); b. "The Lord spoke to the fish and it vomited ..." (2:10); c. "The Lord God prepared a plant..." (4:6); d. "God prepared a worm..." (4:7); e. "God prepared a vehement east wind..." (4:8). The book of Jonah not only emphasizes God's *grace*, God's *goodness*, and God's *government*, but also God's *greatness*.

 In thinking about the preparation of the fish, not only do we have the *miracle recorded*, we also have the *motive revealed*. The verse stated that the Lord prepared the fish to swallow up Jonah. There have been many men who have gone fishing, but here is an example of a fish who went "manning." Someone says: "Wayne, do you truly believe that Jonah was really swallowed by the whale or great fish?" And the answer is: "Yes, I surely do." And I'd believe it if the Bible said that Jonah swallowed the whale! In fact, I'd believe it if the Bible said that Jonah was swallowed by a gold fish in a fishbowl in my living room! We either believe the fourth word of the Bible or we don't. And if, like me, you believe "In the beginning God . . .", then you won't have any trouble believing anything that the Bible says. I mean, after all, "God that made the world and all things therein" (Acts 17:24) surely would have no problem preparing a whale as Jonah's motel. Would He?

PRESERVATION IN THE FISH (1:17b).

Observe the *place* where he was *contained*. Jonah was inside a fish. The belly of that fish became a classroom where he learned an unforgettable lesson about rebelling against God and running from duty. As we study the Bible, we learn that God has often used unusual places and circumstances to teach people lessons they needed to learn. For example, think about Israel during the period of the Judges, Judah in Babylon, and Nebuchadnezzar in the field with the animals, to name a few (Deut. 28:15; Jer. 25:8-11; Dan. 9:1-5; Dan. 4). Note also the entire book of Judges. Also, as we think about the place where he was contained, we need to note that inside the fish he was about as low as he could go. Actually, Jonah's flight from duty has carried him down, down, down, and down. He went d*own* to Joppa (1:3a); d*own* into the ship (1:3b); d*own* into the sea (1:15) and d*own* into the whale's belly (1:17). Evading divinely assigned tasks never raises a child of God to greater heights. Just as Jonah reached his lowest point in life by running from God, so can we. Notice next the *period* in which he *remained* (1:17b). The text says: "Jonah was in the belly of the fish three days and three nights." The Lord Himself verified this as the time Jonah was there. He further stated that Jonah's stay was a type of His own stay for three days and nights in the heart of the earth (Matt. 12:40). Therefore the time that Jonah was in the whale's belly was a hidden prophecy of the Lord's own resurrection. Paul, in writing about the gospel that he preached, stated that Christ rose again the third day according to the scriptures (1 Cor. 15:1-4). One of the scriptures which predicted His resurrection on the *third day* is Jonah 1:17. (See also Hosea 6:1-2.) Also, we need to observe that the period in which Jonah remained as well as his deliverance from the fish was "a sign to the Ninevites" (Lk. 11:30). This means that the people of Nineveh had knowledge of the prophet's deliverance from the great fish. Now we can better understand why the people of Nineveh listened to him when he started preaching. This should also help us realize our responsibility when it comes to listening to the one who is "greater than Jonah" (Lk. 11:32). Jesus was a greater *man* than Jonah. His miracle is a greater *miracle* than was Jonah's. And His message is a greater *message* than was Jonah's. This means that our responsibility to hear and heed is greater than that of Nineveh.

In this final lesson in chapter one we have studied about *the fish*. The *preparation* of the fish as well as Jonah's *preservation* in the fish. In this chapter we have seen Jonah *rebelling*. In the next chapter we will see Jonah *repenting*.

DISCUSSION QUESTIONS

LESSON 3

1. How do we know that the fish that swallowed Jonah was no ordinary fish?

2. How can we prove from the New Testament that the story of Jonah and the whale was an actual occurrence?

3. Name and discuss some of the other miraculous events of the Old Testament that are verified and supported in the New Testament.

4. Is it possible to believe the New Testament and not believe the Old Testament? Explain.

5. Name and discuss some other instances where God used unusual places or circumstances to teach people lessons they needed to learn.

6. Discuss how running from God led to a downward path for Jonah. How does this compare to the path of the prodigal son in Luke 15?

7. Discuss the passage in 1 Corinthians 15:4 in light of Jonah 1:17.

8. Besides the one found in the book of Jonah, what other Old Testament passage may refer to the Lord's resurrection on the *third* day?

9. What is indicated by the fact that Jonah was a sign to the Ninevites? How was Jesus a sign to His generation? (See Luke 11:29-30; Matthew 12:39-40.)

10. Name some of the ways that Jesus is greater than Jonah. (See Luke 11:32.)

CHAPTER TWO

JONAH REPENTING
(Running to God)

I. THE VENTURE (2:1-3). He ventures to pray.

A. The Change in His Position (2:1).
  1. The person to whom he prayed (v.1a).
  2. The place wherein he stayed (v.1b).

B. The Cause of His Submission (2:2).
  1. His trouble—his affliction caused his fear (v.2c).
  2. His trust—he knew the Lord would hear (v.2b).

C. The Creator of His Condition (2:3).
  1. He recognizes the source (v.3a).
  2. He remembers the course (v.3b)

II. THE VOW (2:4-9). He vows to pay.

A. He Reveals His Expectation (2:4).
  1. His failure caused him to be cast out (v.4a).
  2. His faith caused him to turn about (v.4b).

B. He Reviews His Preservation (2:5-6).
  1. The grave destruction was all around (vv.5-6a).
  2. The great deliverance that he found (v.6b).

C. He Renews His Dedication (2:7-9a).
  1. He remembers and decides to pray (v.7).
  2. He renounces and vows to pay (vv.8-9a).

D. He Recognizes His Salvation (2:9b).
  1. The sureness is expressed.
  2. The source is confessed.

III. THE VOMIT (2:10). He's vomited away.

A. Jehovah Voices His Command (2:10a).
  1. The order was Jonah's wish.
  2. The object was the fish.

B. Jonah's Vomited Out on the Land (2:10b).
  1. The parting—the fish couldn't keep him down.
  2. The person—the prophet Jonah was safe and sound.
  3. The place—Jonah's standing on dry ground.

LESSON 4

SCRIPTURE READING
(Jonah 2:1-3)

FROM INSIDE THE FISH JONAH *prayed to the Lord his God.* *² He said: "In my distress I called to the Lord, and he answered me. From deep in the realm of the dead I called for help, and you listened to my cry. ³ You hurled me into the depths, into the very heart of the seas, and the currents swirled about me; all your waves and breakers swept over me.* (NIV)

LESSON 4

THE VENTURE
(He ventures to pray)
Jonah 2:1-3

IN CHAPTER ONE WE SAW Jonah *rebelling* and running *from* God. We know the *cause* of his disobedience—he had the wrong attitude toward God's word and the people of Nineveh. We know the *course* of his disobedience—he went down, down, down, down until he got about as low down as he could get. We saw the *consequences* of his disobedience—he lost his influence for good and his desire to pray, he put other people's lives in danger, and he was swallowed by the whale. In chapter two we're going to see Jonah *repenting* and running *to* God. His disobedience led to his distress which leads to his decision to do better. It was his *venture to pray* in verses 1-3 that led to his *vow to pay* in verses 4-9 which caused him to be *vomited away* in verse ten. As we think about his venture to pray, I want us to notice the change in his position, the cause of his submission, and the creator of his condition.

THE CHANGE IN HIS POSITION.

The main thing we notice in chapter two is the change in Jonah's position. He moves from a position of rebellion to a position of repentance. The text says: "Then Jonah prayed." This indicates his repentance and change of disposition. Note first the *person to whom he prayed.* He prayed "to the Lord his God." In spite of the rebellious attitude he manifested earlier, the Lord was still *his* God. Jonah was truly a man of great faith. He not only believed in the Lord, but he also believed that his God could hear him even from a fish's belly and reward him. (See Hebrews 11:6.) Note also the *place wherein he stayed.* He was still in the fish's belly when he prayed. When he was in the ship he was sleeping, but now that he is in the belly he starts praying. Isn't that exactly what we do many times? We wait until we get into a predicament that we can't get out of and then we pray. But Jesus said, "Men always ought to pray" (Lk. 18:1), not just when we get ourselves in a difficult position. (See 1 Thessalonians 5:17.) But how about us? Is prayer something we use only when you get into a tight spot? Is it a privilege or a pain? A blessing or a bore? A comfort or a chore? In other words, do we still pray when things go right, or do we only pray when we get in a tight spot? Notice too that the place wherein he stayed is the place from which he prayed. That shows, clearly and convincingly, that a person's physical position when he prays doesn't matter. In the Bible, people prayed standing (Mk.

11:25); kneeling (Acts 20:36); appearing before a king (Neh. 2:4); lying on a bed facing a wall (Isa. 38:1-2); falling on his face (Matt. 26:39); looking up to heaven (Jn. 17:1), and from a whale's belly. From these examples, as well as Jonah, we learn that a man can pray with a sincere heart regardless of his physical position.

THE CAUSE OF HIS SUBMISSION (2:2).

Notice that his *trouble* was the *cause of his submission*. Jonah said, "I cried out because of my affliction." His *affliction caused his fear.* The Lord had chastened him and the discipline had worked. And even though it wasn't pleasant, it was profitable. It helped Jonah see the need of doing what the Lord said. *Affliction* sometimes helps us in our *affection*. Affliction not only helped Jonah, but it has also helped many others. The psalmist said, "Before I was afflicted I went astray: but now have I kept your word" (Ps. 119:67). Again he wrote, "It is good for me that I have been afflicted; that I might learn your statutes" (Ps. 119:71). Even today God may use trouble and persecution to help us be better, especially when we step out of line like Jonah did. (See Romans 5:3; James 1:2-3; and Hebrews 12:5-11.) Notice too that Jonah's *trust* was also a cause of his submission. The text says, "He answered me." Jonah knew the Lord would hear. His affliction caused his fear and *he knew the Lord would hear.* This knowledge led to his submission. I'm glad He heard Jonah. Because if He could hear Jonah way down in the sea, then

He can hear you and He can hear me. (See 1 Peter 3:12; Matthew 7:7-8; and 1 John 5:14.) Actually, the cure for care is casting (1 Pet. 5:7). The path to peace is prayer (Phil. 4:6-7). We know that we can talk to Him because He's always there (Lk. 18:1; 1 Pet. 3:12).

THE CREATOR OF HIS CONDITION (2:3).

Jonah recognizes the *source* or creator of his affliction. Note his references to those situations and things that oppressed him: "You cast me into the deep;" "Your billows;" "Your waves;" etc. Jonah was definitely distressed because of his rebellion and he recognized God as the source of his affliction. It was the Lord who helped Jonah see the light even though Jonah was refusing to do what was right. Jonah acknowledged that God had cast him into the deep. The sailors were only His instruments. God cares enough to correct. He is not only a God of protection (Ps. 46:1), He is also a God of correction (Heb. 12:9; 2 Tim. 3:16-17). He also remembers the *course* that he traveled. He remembered how he was "cast into the deep" and how "the floods surrounded" him about and how the "waves passed over" him. From this we learn that God's discipline is not always easy. Jonah had it rough in the sea. But God disciplines His disciples to make us more dedicated. He seeks to make us better, not bitter. He helped Jonah and He will also help us. He chastens us for our profit, that we might be partakers of His holiness (Heb. 12:10). And it is not always easy or pleasant. In fact, "no chastening seems to be joyful for the present, but painful, nevertheless, afterward it yields the peaceful fruit of righteousness to those who have been trained by it" (Heb. 12:11). God's discipline is His training course.

In this second chapter Jonah is *repenting*. In these first three verses we have discussed the *venture* as he ventures to pray. It was *the venture* in verses 1-3 that led to *the vow* in verses 4-9 which will be the subject of our next study.

DISCUSSION QUESTIONS

LESSON 4

1. What does Jonah do in chapter 2 that indicates he is running *to* God instead of *from* Him?

2. What does this prove concerning his faith?

3. How is Jonah's prayer like many Christians' prayers today?

4. Discuss some of the ideas that men have concerning posture in prayer. How does Jonah help us in this matter?

5. How can trouble and affliction be profitable? Could this be one of the reasons that James said, "Count it all joy when you fall into various trials" (James 1:2)? Discuss.

6. Read and discuss some of the verses in the New Testament that assure us that God will hear us when we pray.

7. How do we know for sure that God had "loaded the lots" to make sure that Jonah was cast into the sea?

8. Whom did God use to help correct Jonah? Cite other Old Testament examples where God used unbelievers as instruments to chastise His people. (See Isaiah 10:5-7.) Discuss New Testament examples. (See Hebrews 12:5-13.) Suggest some ways He may use unbelievers today to chastise us?

9. Why did God correct Jonah? Why does He correct us?

10. What does Hebrews 12 teach about the pleasantness of God's chastisement? How is this illustrated by the example of Jonah?

LESSON 5

SCRIPTURE READING
(Jonah 2:4-9)

THEN I SAID, 'O LORD, *you have driven me from your presence. Yet I will look once more toward your holy Temple.'*
⁵ "I sank beneath the waves,
and the waters closed over me.
Seaweed wrapped itself around my head.
⁶ I sank down to the very roots of the mountains.
I was imprisoned in the earth,
whose gates lock shut forever.
But you, O LORD my God,
snatched me from the jaws of death!
⁷ As my life was slipping away,
I remembered the LORD.
And my earnest prayer went out to you
in your holy Temple.
⁸ Those who worship false gods
turn their backs on all God's mercies.
⁹ But I will offer sacrifices to you with songs of

*praise, and I will fulfill all my vows.
For my salvation comes from the* LORD *alone."
(NLT)*

LESSON 5

THE VOW
(He vows to pay)
Jonah 2:4-9

IN THIS STUDY WE LOOK at Jonah's vow to pay. As Jonah *ventures to pray* in verses 1-3, he *vows to pay* in verses 4-9. Actually, his prayer contained the vow in verse 9: "I will fulfill all my vows." This study deals with the statements leading up to and including that vow. In this section he reveals his expectation; reviews his preservation, renews his dedication, and recognizes his salvation.

HE REVEALS HIS EXPECTATION (2:4).

His *failure* caused him to be *cast out* (2:4a). In verse four, Jonah reveals how he expects to look again toward God's Temple. Both repentance and hope are expressed here. His failure caused him to be cast out. He admitted the he had been driven from the Lord's presence. He had failed because of his rebellion. His *faith* caused him to *turn about* (2:4b). He said: "I will look once more toward your holy Temple." The fact that he was still alive in the fish's belly assured him that he would again look toward the holy Temple of God's presence. It also caused him to have the change of heart necessary to be back again in the Lord's favorable presence. He had definitely failed. But his failure was not fatal or final. Why? Because he *faced his failure with faith*. This is what we need to learn to do (Rom. 15:4). This is at least one of the reasons that Samson is in the great faith chapter in Hebrews 11. He faced his failure with faith (Heb. 11:32). Also, some of God's greatest servants failed at times, yet they faced their failures with faith. For example, think about: Noah (Gen. 9:20-21; Ezek. 14:14; Heb. 11:7); Abraham (Gen. 12:12-13; 20:13; Rom. 4:11; Heb. 11:8-10); Moses (Num. 20:7-12; Ps. 106:32-33; Matt. 17:1-5); David (2 Sam. 11-12; Ps. 51; Ps. 32; Acts 13:22); Peter (Matt. 26:69-75; Jn. 21:15-19; Acts 2); John, Mark (Acts 13:13; 15:38; 2 Tim. 4:11); and Jonah. All of us fail at various times in our responsibility to God (2 Chron. 6:36; Eccl. 7:20; Rom. 3:23). But let us learn from Jonah, as well as from other great men of God, that failure doesn't have to be *fatal*. And failure doesn't have to be *final*. We can face our failures with *faith*.

HE REVIEWS HIS PRESERVATION (2:5-6).

Jonah reviews how he was preserved by the Lord. He first tells of the *grave destruction that was all around*. He was compassed about, closed up, wrapped up, and seemingly about to give up. He was to the point of saying: "The earth with its bars closed behind me for ever." His situation looked hopeless and he was helpless to do anything about it. But then notice the *great deliverance that he found.* Jonah said: "But you, O Lord my God, snatched me from the jaws of death!" With his hope almost gone, the Lord didn't leave him all alone, but rather delivered him from dying. Anytime a situation seems hopeless we need to remember that we serve a God who is able to do exceedingly abundantly above all that we ask or think according to the power that works in us (Eph. 3:20). Many times we get into situations spiritually that we just can't seem to get out of. We may get so wrapped up in the world and in sin that the situation looks completely hopeless (Jude 1:23). It is then that we need to learn from Jonah that even though grave destruction maybe all around, great deliverance can be found.

HE RENEWS HIS DEDICATION (2:7-9c).

After reviewing his preservation, Jonah renews his dedication. Actually, his preservation led to his dedication. First, he *remembers and decides to pray.* He remembers the Lord and this is what caused him to pray. But notice *when* he remembered: "When my soul fainted within me." Jonah was like the prodigal son who, when he was about to "perish with hunger," remembered his father's house (Lk. 15:17). Think about *why* he remembered. He had known about the blessing of the Lord before—when he was doing right. Like the prodigal who remembered that the "hired servants of my father's house have bread enough and to spare" (Lk. 15:17). Think also about *what* he remembered. What did Jonah remember about the Lord that caused him to pray? He could have remembered the Lord's *might*. He knew about the Lord's great power for He had "made the sea and the dry land" (1:9). He could have remembered the Lord's *message*. The Lord had given him a message that he was to preach to Nineveh. But he obviously remembered the Lord's *mercy*. This is undoubtedly what caused him to pray. He knew that God was a gracious God and merciful (4:2), and that in running from God he had forsaken his own mercy (2:8). It was remembering the father's goodness and mercy that caused the prodigal to decide to "arise and go to my father" and say to him "I have sinned" (Lk. 15:17-19). Today when we are in misery because of sin, we too need to be reminded of the mercy of the Savior. The goodness of God can indeed lead one to repentance (Rom. 2:4) as is demonstrated in the case of Jonah.

Not only does he remember and decide to pray, he also *renounces and vows to pay* (2:8,9c). He renounces lying vanities in verse eight by saying, "Those who worship false gods turn their backs on all God's mercies." False gods and idols are valueless or worthless. This could include both ideas and idols. In chapter one Jonah had followed his own worthless way rather than God's righteous commandment. He therefore had forsaken the mercy that could have been his had he remained faithful. He vows to pay by saying: "But I will offer sacrifices to you with songs of praise and I will fulfill my vows." He made a promise to the Lord and kept it. But how about us? Have we made promises to the Lord that we haven't kept? What about when we were sick, in bad circumstances, or trying to convert someone. Did we make promises to the Lord? Have we paid that which we have vowed?

HE RECOGNIZES HIS SALVATION (2:9b).

The *sureness is expressed* as Jonah says, "Salvation is of the Lord." There is, at this point, no doubt in his mind concerning his salvation. Like Paul in 2 Timothy 1:12, Jonah knew and knew that he knew. The *source* is *confessed*. Jonah confesses that his salvation is of the Lord. The only source of salvation is Jehovah and Jonah had to learn this the hard way. Jonah knew now by experience that God is the only source of salvation for men who are helpless and hopeless. Hopefully, we today will not have to go through what Jonah did in order to recognize that salvation is of the Lord. Today Jesus is the salvation of God that all men need to see (Lk. 3:6). He is the way, the truth, and life (Jn. 14:6). Neither is there salvation in any other (Acts 4:12). He is the author of eternal salvation to all who believe.

In this study we have discussed the *vow* that Jonah made to the Lord. As he *ventured to pray*, he *vowed to pay*. And this brings us to our final study in chapter two which concerns *the vomit*.

DISCUSSION QUESTIONS

LESSON 5

1. What is expressed in the statement of Jonah: "I will look again toward Your holy temple"?

2. Why was not Jonah's failure fatal or final?

3. Name at least one of the reasons that Samson is in the great faith chapter of Hebrews 11.

4. Name some other great men and women in the Old Testament who faced their failures with faith.

5. Give similar examples from the New Testament.

6. What is the primary lesson we learn from all these examples. Why is this lesson so important to us?

7. What New Testament passage can serve as a great source of hope when situations in our lives look hopeless?

8. What do you think that Jonah remembered most about the Lord that caused him to repent and pray? Discuss.

9. Discuss the importance of keeping the vows that we make to the Lord.

10. Explain: "Salvation is from the Lord alone."

LESSON 6

SCRIPTURE READING
(Jonah 2:10)

AND THE LORD SPOKE TO *the fish, and it vomited Jonah out upon the dry land. (ESV)*

LESSON 6

THE VOMIT
(He's vomited away)
Jonah 2:10

IN THIS STUDY WE WILL notice how Jonah is vomited away. As he *ventures to pray* he *vows to pay* and now he's going to be *vomited away*. We will see how Jehovah voices His command and Jonah's vomited out on the land.

JEHOVAH VOICES HIS COMMAND (2:10a).

The Lord gave an order to the fish, which was exactly what Jonah had wished. The text says the Lord spoke to the fish. This is what Jonah wished for. He wanted to be delivered from the fish's belly. He got what he wanted when he changed his will. He was rewarded after he repented. And he not only got what he wanted, he also got what he needed. Today all of us are bound to sin (Jn. 8:34) just as Jonah was trapped in the whale's belly. And we need to be delivered. But in order for that to happen, we too must have a change of mind like Jonah did. The Jews in Acts two were like Jonah in Jonah two. They also got what they wanted as well as what they needed, but they had to repent and be baptized in the name of Jesus as a demonstration of their faith in Him before they received it (Acts 2:37-41). The *object* was the *fish*. The text says the Lord "spoke to the fish." This is really not surprising to those who believe and are familiar with the Bible. Jehovah has voiced His command on numerous occasions with amazing results. In fact, the first chapter of Genesis sets the tone for the rest of the Bible as again and again it emphasizes the power in God's spoken word. At least ten times in Genesis one, Moses makes specific reference to what God said. Actually, Genesis 1:9 could really sum it up when Moses wrote, "God said... and it was so." In Psalms 33:6-9 the Psalmist said plainly, "By the word of the Lord the heavens were made; and all the host of them by the breath of his mouth... For He spoke and it was done; He commanded and it stood fast." (See also Hebrews 11:3.) It is what the Lord spoke that was the basis of *creation*. His word is "living and powerful ..." (Heb. 4:12). What the Lord spoke was not only the basis of creation, it is also the basis of *revelation* (2 Tim. 3:16-17; 2 Pet. 1:20-21). The Lord chose the very words that the inspired men used in revealing the gospel to man (1 Cor. 2:8-14; Eph. 3:3-5). And not only is what the Lord spoke the basis of creation and revelation, it is also the basis of *salvation* (Heb. 2:3). Jesus spoke the words of eternal life (Jn. 6:68). What God "spoke" was the basis of Jonah's salvation and deliverance from the predicament that his sin had gotten him into. And what the Lord has spoken is also the basis of our salvation and deliverance from what our sins have gotten us into. What the Lord spoke saved Jonah from the whale, and what the Lord has spoken can save us from hell. (See James 1:21.)

JONAH'S VOMITED OUT ON THE LAND (2:10b).

Jehovah voices His command and ***Jonah is vomited out on the land.*** The fish could not keep Jonah down once the Lord had spoken. Jonah and the fish parted company. Vomiting is never pleasant. I almost get sick myself if I'm around someone who starts vomiting. But we need to learn that everything in the Bible is not pleasant and pleasing. God calls things as they are and sometimes what He says is not pleasant. The Bible tells us about dogs eating the flesh of Jezebel after she was splattered and run over (2 Kings 9:30-37). A woman boiled her son and ate him (2 Kings 6:28-29). Job having sore boils from his feet to his crown with running sores and worms (Job 2:7; 7:5). Judas who fell headlong into a field and burst asunder in the midst and all his entrails gushed out (Acts 1:18). A man being eaten of worms (Acts 12:23). Babies being slaughtered (Matt. 2), as well as numerous other unpleasant and repulsive happenings. When God described the abominations of Jerusalem in Ezekiel 16, He used language that was plain and pointed but not pleasant. When

Peter describes a backslider in 2 Peter 2:20-22, he compares him to a dog eating his own vomit. The lukewarm in the Laodicean Church caused the Lord to say: "I will vomit you out of my mouth" (Rev. 3:17). When God describes the punishment of the wicked, it is not pleasing or pleasant. He says it will be "everlasting punishment" (Matt. 25:46) in "everlasting fire" (Matt. 25:41), where there will be "tribulation and anguish" (Rom. 2:9), "torment" (Lk. 16:23-25), and "wailing and gnashing of teeth" (Matt. 8:12; 13:42). Paul said: "Behold therefore the goodness and severity of God..." (Rom. 11:22). Reading and thinking about His goodness and mercy is both pleasing and pleasant. But we must not overlook the severity with which He deals with those who die in sin without Jesus.

The fish couldn't keep him down. The prophet Jonah was safe and sound. A little girl was asked: "What is the main lesson we learn from Jonah being vomited from the fish?" She answered: "You can't keep a good man down!" (See Psalm 37:23-24.) Jonah was the same person in many respects who had been swallowed by the fish, but now he was also a different person. His relationship to the Lord was different because he is now ready to run *with* the Lord instead of *from* Him. He is now a converted person—changed from the way he was. The Lord has helped him change. His condition at this point reminds us of those who are born again today. Although they are the same people outwardly, they are different inwardly. The touch of the Master's hand changes people (1 Cor. 6:9-11; Rev. 1:17). Paul stated it like this: "If anyone is in Christ he is a new creation, old things have passed away, behold, all things have become new" (2 Cor. 5:17). The Jews who were converted in Acts 2 were the same outwardly yet different inwardly. The same is true with the Samaritans (Acts 8); the eunuch (Acts 8); Paul (Acts 9); Cornelius (Acts 10); Lydia (Acts 16); the jailor (Acts 16); the Corinthians (Acts 18; 1 Cor. 6:9-11); the Ephesians (Acts 19:1-5); and all others who believe the gospel from the heart (Rom. 6:16-18). Today any person can come to Jesus (Jn. 6:37) and be buried in baptism and raised to walk in *newness* of life (Rom. 6:3-4). He will be the same person outwardly, but different inwardly.

The text says that the fish vomited out Jonah on dry land (2:10). Jonah is now standing on dry land. He is now where the Lord wants him to be and he is ready to do the Lord's bidding. Jonah is now in the place where he can do what the Lord wants done. A person who is in Christ today is also in the place where God can use him/her in His service. (See Hebrews 12:28 and Ephesians 2:8-10.) As the people of God, we need to be willing to do what we can with what we have while we are here. (Matt. 25:14-30; 1 Cor. 15:58; Tit. 3:1.) For who knows whether we are come to the kingdom for such a time as this (Esther 4:14)?

In this final study in chapter two, we have studied about the vomit. It was his *venture to pray* that led to his *vow to pay* which led to his being *vomited away*.

In this chapter Jonah has been *repenting* and running *to* God. In our next study we will begin chapter three and see him *responding* and running *with* God.

DISCUSSION QUESTIONS

LESSON 6

1. At what point did Jonah get what he wanted and needed?

2. What comparison can we make between Jonah in chapter two with the Jews in Acts two?

3. Discuss the power in the word of God as is illustrated in His speaking to the fish and His creation of the world.

4. What passages in the New Testament prove that God selected the very words that the inspired men used in making known His revelation to man?

5. What is the basis or foundation of our salvation?

6. Is everything in the Bible pleasing and pleasant to read? Discuss.

7. How does Peter describe a backslider in 2 Peter 2:20-21?

8. How does God describe the punishment of the wicked?

9. Explain how the gospel of Christ changes a person.

10. What does God expect of one who has been born again?

CHAPTER THREE

JONAH RESPONDING
(Running with God)

I. THE MESSAGE (3:1-4). The message is presented.

A. A Revealed Message (3:1-3).
   1. The commission to the prophet (vv.1-2a).
   2. The content of the preaching (v.2b).
   3. The city to be punished (v.3).

B. A Relevant Message (3:4).
   1. The prophet gets started (v.4a).
   2. The period is stated (v.4b).
   3. The punishment is sure (v.4c).

C. A Rough Message (3:4).
   1. No mercy in this message, only misery (v.4b).
   2. No pardon in this preaching, only punishment   (v.4c).

II. THE MOURNING (3:5-9). The mourners repented.

   A. The Repentance That Is Seen (3:5-6).
      1. It started with the people (v.5).
      2. It spread to the palace (v.6).

   B. The Requirement of the King (3:7-8).
      1. The declaration (v.7a).
      2. The demonstration (7b-8).

   C. The Reason for these Things (3:9).
      1. To appease the anger (v.9).
      2. To avoid the danger (v.9b).

III. THE MERCY (3:10). The mercy is extended.

   A. God Recognizes Their Sincerity (3:10a).
      1. He saw how they tried.
      2. He saw how they turned.

   B. God Relents of the Severity (3:10b).
      1. He retracted the punishment.
      2. He reacted with pardon.

LESSON 7

SCRIPTURE READING
(Jonah 3:1-4)

THEN THE WORD OF THE *Lord came to Jonah the second time, saying,* ² *"Arise, go to Nineveh, that great city, and call out against it the message that I tell you."* ³ *So Jonah arose and went to Nineveh, according to the word of the* LORD. NOW NINEVEH WAS AN EXCEEDINGLY GREAT CITY, THREE DAYS' JOURNEY IN BREADTH. ⁴ *Jonah began to go into the city, going a day's journey. And he called out, "Yet forty days, and Nineveh shall be overthrown!"* **(ESV)**

LESSON 7

THE MESSAGE
(The message is presented)
Jonah 3:1-4

IN CHAPTER ONE WE SAW Jonah *rebelling* and running *from* God. In chapter two we saw him *repenting* and running *to* God. Now in chapter three we're going to see him *responding* and running *with* God. His disobedience in chapter one led to his distress in chapter two which leads to his discourse in chapter three. In this first study in chapter three, we're going to notice *the message*. It is the *message* in verses 1-4 that lead to the *mourning* in verses 5-9 which leads to the *mercy* in verse 10. After the message was presented, the mourners repented, and the mercy was extended. As we think about the message of Jonah to Nineveh, I want us to notice three things about it. It was a revealed message, a relevant message, and a rough message.

A REVEALED MESSAGE (3:1-4).

Observe the *commission* to the *prophet* (3:1-2). The text says that the word of the Lord came to Jonah the second time. Here was another commission from God to preach to Nineveh. God is the God of the second chance. Jeremiah 18: 3-4 shows that God gives a second chance. In verse four a vessel was *made*, then it was *marred*, and then it was *mended*. The mending demonstrates being given another chance. Abraham (Gen. 12); David (2 Sam. 11-12; Ps. 51 & 32); Peter (Matt. 26:69-75; Acts 2:14); and Jonah are all examples of men given another chance. And Jonah made the best of his second chance because he arose and went to Nineveh. In verse two God said: "arise and go," and in verse three the text says he "arose and went." This reminds us of Philip in Acts 8. He was commissioned to "arise and go" (Acts 8:26) and he too "arose and went" (Acts 8:27). Later, he was told to "go near and overtake this chariot" and he "ran" to him (Acts 8:29-30). This is the attitude we need in the church today since we too have been commissioned to go preach to others (Matt. 28:19; Mk. 16:15). And if we had more saints who would *run*, more souls could be *won*. Jesus wants "laborers" in His vineyard, not "loafers" (Matt. 20:1). We can't go to heaven in a rocking chair because the Lord doesn't allow any lazy folks there (Eccl. 9:10; Rom. 12:11). Jesus said: "The harvest is truly plentiful but the laborers are few" (Matt. 9:37). He didn't say: "The harvest is finished and the laborers are through." We need to start standing on the promises rather than just sitting on the premises. If we want to make progress like Jonah did, we must be ready to preach like Jonah was. (See Romans 1:15.) Like Isaiah, we need to say, "Here am I; send me" (Isa. 6:8). And we need to do like Jonah, who when God said "arise and go," he "arose and went." Notice also the *content* of the *preaching* (3:2b). Observe that God told Jonah to "preach to it the message that I tell you." The content of his message was to be what the Lord had said on the subject. Paul told Timothy the same thing in 2Timothy 4:2 when he said, "Preach the word." That is, preach the preaching that the Lord bids us. Preachers should not preach anything other than that which the Lord bids us to preach (2 Jn. 1:9-10). We don't have any business preaching about men, messages, or methods that the Lord has not bidden us to preach (2 Tim. 3:16-17). But we do need to preach the preaching that He bids us to preach about such things as the inspiration of the scriptures (2 Tim. 3:16-17). We must preach about the soul, sin, and separation (Matt. 10:28; Rom. 6:23; Isa. 59:1-2). People must know about the Savior (Matt. 1:21); salvation (Rom. 1:16), and the Spirit (Rom. 8:9-14). They need messages about sanctification (Jn. 17:17; 1 Cor. 1:2), service (Heb. 12:28), and steadfastness (1 Cor. 15:58). They need to understand the importance of studying (2 Tim. 2:15), and making supplication (1 Tim. 2:1). We all need to understand the importance of singing (Eph. 5:19), support (1 Cor. 16:1-2), and the Lord's supper (1 Cor. 11:23-33). We need to know about how Christians are saved (2 Tim. 1:9); sure (1 Jn. 5:11-12), and secure in Christ (Jn. 10:27-29). And we need to also recognize that all preaching is not pleasant. Sometimes the preaching that the Lord bids us involves convincing and rebuking as well as exhorting (2 Tim. 4:1-2). Like Jonah, there are times when we must preach against certain things and point out that sin must be punished (3:4). Remember we cannot always be mild-mannered preachers who preach mild-mannered sermons to mild-mannered people on how to be more mild mannered.

The *commission* to the *prophet* was about the *city* to be *punished*. When Nineveh is first mentioned in this book, it is called "that great city" (1:2). But in this chapter it is called an "exceedingly" great city (3:2). It was exceedingly great in *size*. This is what Jonah had in mind in verse three. It was an exceedingly great city of three days' journey which probably means that it was so large that it would take Jonah three days to go through it preaching (3:4a). It was also exceedingly great in *sinfulness*. This is why Jonah was sent there in the first place. Their wickedness had come up before God (1:2). It had gotten so bad that God would tolerate them no longer. It was also exceedingly great in *souls*. In chapter 4:11, we learn that there were more than one hundred and twenty thousand persons who may not have reached the age of accountability. If this is true then there were multitudes of adults who needed to be converted. Many cities in America, as well as other nations, are also exceedingly great in size, sinfulness, and souls. And they too need to hear the preaching that the Lord has told us to preach. When

Paul was in the great city of Athens, "his spirit was provoked within him when he saw that the city was given over to idols" (Acts 17:16). When Jesus came to Jerusalem for the last time, "He saw the city, and wept over it" (Lk. 19:41). How do we see cities today? Do we only see the size? What about the sinfulness? What about the souls?

A RELEVANT MESSAGE.

Not only was it a *revealed* message, it was also a *relevant* message. In verse four the *prophet gets started*. He enters the city a day's journey preaching: "Yet forty days and Nineveh shall be overthrown." A good example of the results of true repentance is seen here. Jonah changed his mind which brought about a change in his actions. When the word first came to Jonah, he "arose to flee to Tarshish" (1:3), but now he "arose and went to Nineveh." Repentance results in a change of one's actions. The prophet gets started because his message was relevant. This is seen when the *period is stated*. Jonah said: "Yet forty days," which demonstrates that the message dealt with a matter at hand. His preaching was to the point and important to the Ninevites. There were many other truths that Jonah could have preached, but this is the message that was most needed at that particular time. It is not enough to simply preach the truth. We must preach the truth that is needed (Acts 20:20-27). Preaching the truth in love (Eph. 4:15) demands that we preach what people need to hear whether it's what they want to hear or not (2 Tim. 4:1-2; Matt.

23). The period is stated because the *punishment* is *sure*. Jonah preached: "Yet forty days, and Nineveh shall be overthrown" (3:4b). In only forty days the Ninevites would be destroyed, and they needed to know it. We learn from Jonah that people need to be warned of God's coming judgment on sin (1 Thess. 1:10). Enoch, the seventh from Adam, warned the people of his day that God was coming to "execute judgment upon all..." (Jude 1:14-15). People today need to be warned that God's punishment for sin is sure. He is coming to "take vengeance on those who do not know God and who do not obey the gospel of our Lord Jesus Christ" (2 Thess. 1:6-9). Preaching about God's punishment will not only cause sinners to realize their need of forgiveness, but it will also help saints realize the importance of persuading the lost to believe in Jesus (2 Cor. 5:10-11).

A ROUGH MESSAGE.

Not only was Jonah's message revealed and relevant, it was also *rough*. There was no *mercy* in this *message*. How would you like to have Jonah's job? He is a foreigner in a strange city among the enemies of his people with a message of doom. All he had was a message of gloom and doom. Today we have a message of grace and glory. Think about it, there was no offer of *pardon* in this *preaching*. There was no promise or hope connected with it. It was only "yet forty days and Nineveh shall be overthrown." Today we have the gospel of Christ which includes "glad tidings of good things" (Rom. 10:15) as well as hope and assurance. Do we preach it to strangers? Would we preach it to our enemies? Do we even bother to preach it to our friends, neighbors, or kinfolks? Jonah's preaching will condemn some at the judgment (Matt. 12:41). He had a message that was rough on those he preached to while we have a message that relieves those we preach to, if they believe it. We have a message of mercy and a gospel of peace that people today need to hear just as much as Nineveh needed to hear the message Jonah had for them. May we all be encouraged by Jonah's action to get on with sharing it with others.

In this third chapter, Jonah is *responding.* In these first three verses we have studied about *the message* as the message is presented. It was this *message* in verses 1-3 that brought about the *mourning* in verses 4-9 which will be the subject of our next study.

DISCUSSION QUESTIONS

LESSON 7

1. In chapter one, Jonah is running *from* God. In chapter two, he is running *to* God. How is he running in chapter three?

2. How can we prove that God is a God of the second chance?

3. Discuss Jeremiah 18:3-4.

4. Explain how Jonah's attitude in this chapter is an example of how Christians should react today.

5. What was the content of Jonah's preaching?

6. How does Jonah's message serve as an example of how our preaching should be today?

7. Discuss some of the important subjects that must be covered in our preaching today.

8. In what ways was Nineveh an "exceedingly great city." How should we see cities today?

9. Discuss the difference between preaching the truth and in preaching the truth that is needed. Give some Bible examples of preaching the truth that is needed.

10. Describe the major difference between the message Jonah preached to Nineveh and the gospel that we are to preach to the world.

LESSON 8

SCRIPTURE READING
(Jonah 3:5-9)

So THE PEOPLE OF NINEVEH *believed God, and proclaimed a fast, and put on sackcloth, from the greatest of them even to the least of them.* ⁶*For word came unto the king of Nineveh, and he arose from his throne, and he laid his robe from him, and covered him with sackcloth, and sat in ashes.* ⁷*And he caused it to be proclaimed and published through Nineveh by the decree of the king and his nobles, saying, Let neither man nor beast, herd nor flock, taste any thing: let them not feed, nor drink water:* ⁸*But let man and beast be covered with sackcloth, and cry mightily unto God: yea, let them turn every one from his evil way, and from the violence that is in their hands.* ⁹*Who can tell if God will turn and repent, and turn away from his fierce anger, that we perish not? (NKJV)*

LESSON 8

THE MOURNING
(The mourners repented)
Jonah 3:5-9

IN THIS SECOND LESSON FROM chapter three, we study about the *mourning*. The *message* of the *prophet* brought about the *mourning* of the *people*.. When the message was presented, the mourners repented. As we study this section we will notice the repentance that is seen, the requirement of the king, and the reason for these things.

THE REPENTANCE THAT IS SEEN.

The change *started* with the *people* (3:5). The text says: "So the people of Nineveh believed God" and they proclaimed a fast. Their prompt and extreme action clearly shows their repentance. They not only believed, but they demonstrated that belief by fasting and putting on sackcloth. Jesus said that the people of Nineveh "repented at the preaching of Jonah" (Matt. 12:41). Jesus also said that Jonah was a "sign to the Ninevites" (Lk. 11:30) which clearly indicates that they had learned in some way of Jonah's experience in the fish. This helps us understand why they would listen as they did. Also, we must never underestimate the power of God's word. His word is indeed "living and powerful" (Heb. 4:12). "The law of the Lord is perfect, converting the soul" (Ps. 19:7). And today we have the gospel which is "the *power* of God to salvation" (Rom.1:16). We must never forget or overlook the fact that God's word can change drunkards, fornicators, thieves, and such like. (See 1 Corinthians 6:9-11.) It started with the people, but then it *spread* to the p*alace* (3:6). The repentance that started with the people reached the king. Then word came to the king of Nineveh "and he covered himself with sackcloth and sat in ashes" (3:6). Now who would have thought for a moment that the king would respond by repenting? Not I! But he did. This illustrates that we must be careful about making decisions for others. For example, we might say: I would try to teach the mayor, but a man in his position wouldn't listen. I would try to teach this certain religious person who is in a false religion, but he's too dedicated to what he believes to listen. I would teach my brother, uncle, neighbor, friend, or boss, but they wouldn't listen. Let us learn from the reaction of the king that you really never know who will listen and who will not. Jesus said: "Go ye into all the world and preach the gospel to every creature" (Mk. 16:15). He did not say go and preach the gospel to those whom you think will listen. Who would have thought that the Jews (Acts 2);

Paul (Acts 9); the jailor (Acts 16); or the Corinthians (1 Cor. 6:9-11) would have been converted by the gospel? Probably no one. But they were! We need to be careful about trying to make decisions for others. Let's preach the gospel to them and let them decide for themselves. (See 1 Corinthians 2:11.)

THE REQUIREMENT OF THE KING.

Observe first the d*eclaration* (3:7a). The king sends out a decree from both himself and his nobles. He has it published throughout Nineveh. The king was serious about this matter. He even demanded that the animals be involved which would indicate the total repentance of the entire city. This illustrates what one man can do who is in a position of influence. It should help us see the need of trying to convert people who are in a position to influence a lot of others. And while Paul warns us that not many mighty and noble will respond, he did say "not many," rather than "not any" (1 Cor. 1:26). (See also Acts 8:26-39.) Observe second, that the declaration called for a d*emonstration* (3:7b-8). This king demanded both a demonstration and a *departure.* They were to demonstrate their humility and sorrow by fasting and putting on sackcloth. And they were to depart from their evil way and from the violence they were doing. Jesus said that the Ninevites *repented* (Matt. 12:41). The book of Jonah says: "They *turned* from their evil way" (3:10). Therefore, true repentance involves a change in one's action. Biblical repentance is a change of mind which brings about or results in a change in action. If a person has been doing evil and he repents, then he turns from evil just like the Ninevites did. Let us learn from the repentance of the Ninevites that repentance in the heart results in reformation in the life.

THE REASON FOR THESE THINGS.

The reason for the repentance of the people and the requirement of the king was to *appease the anger* of God (3:9). God was angry with the Ninevites because of their sins and was about to bring judgment on them. The psalmist said that God is angry with the wicked every day (Ps. 7:11). Therefore, He is angry with those who practice sin as a way of life today. The reason they wanted to *appease the anger* was so they could *avoid the danger.* They wanted God to turn away from His fierce anger that they perish not. The way for men today to appease His anger, and thus avoid the danger that His judgment will bring on them, is to do like Nineveh did—believe His word and repent of their sins. (See 2 Thessalonians 1:6-9.) Think about how much better we have it today than Nineveh did. They did not know whether God would forgive them or not. They repented not knowing. But today we know that He is ready and willing to forgive all who will come to Him in repentance (2 Pet. 3:9). We know that those who come to Him will not be cast out (Jn. 6:37). We know that He invites all to come (Matt. 11:28-30) and that includes every creature (Mk. 16:15). Also, think how much better we have it today from the standpoint of opportunity. They had one *speaker,* with one *sermon,* who had no *sympathy,* offered no *salvation,* and of course, there was no *sureness* that God would forgive them. The men of Nineveh may rise up in the judgment and condemn a lot of people (Matt. 12:41).

In this study we have discussed the *mourning* of the Ninevites. The *message* in verses 1-4 brought about the *mourning* in verses 5-9 which brings us to the subject of our next study in verse 10, which is the *mercy.*

DISCUSSION QUESTIONS

LESSON 8

1. What did the people of Nineveh do upon hearing Jonah's message?

2. What did Jesus call what the Ninevites did?

3. Discuss the danger in underestimating the power of God's word.

4. Why should we never decide for other people whether they will or will not obey God's word?

5. What did the king of Nineveh do when he heard the message of Jonah?

6. Give a definition and example of Bible repentance.

7. Can a person repent of a sin and continue in willful habitual practice of that sin? Discuss specifically the sins of lying, stealing, and adultery in the context of repentance. How is a person's conduct changed when he repents of these sins?

8. Why did Nineveh repent? Did the Ninevites know that God would forgive them?

9. Find some passages in the New Testament that assure us of God's willingness to forgive all who repent today.

10. Contrast the way God's message was presented to the Ninevites with the way the gospel is presented to the lost today.

LESSON 9

SCRIPTURE READING
(Jonah 3:10)

*W**HEN GOD SAW WHAT THEY did and how they turned from their evil ways, he relented and did not bring on them the destruction he had threatened.* **(NIV)**

LESSON 9

THE MERCY
(The mercy is extended)
Jonah 3:10

IN THIS STUDY WE'RE GOING to see the *mercy extended*. It was the *message* that led to the *mourning* which led to the *mercy*. We will observe how God recognizes their sincerity and how He relents of the severity.

GOD RECOGNIZES THEIR SINCERITY.

Observe that God saw how they *tried*. The text says, "Then God saw their works." He saw how they tried and He heard how they *cried* (v.8). I'm glad that God sees us when we are doing good. His eyes are in every place beholding the evil and the *good* (Prov. 15:3). God knew that Job was doing right and He was proud of him (Job 1:8). Jesus knew about the bad things going on in the church in Laodicea, but He also knew about the good things that were happening in the church in Philadelphia (Rev. 3).

God saw the great *wickedness* of Nineveh according to chapter one, and He also saw the good *works* of Nineveh in chapter three. God saw that they *turned* from their evil way. Heaven is interested in those who repent (Lk. 15:10). Observe also that repentance is an expression of faith. In Jonah 3:5 they *"believed* God" and *"repented* at the preaching of Jonah" (Matt. 12:41). Jonah 3:10 says that God saw that they turned from their evil way because they believed God. Therefore, repentance is a change. It is not simply a decision, but it is a result of faith in the heart that causes change in action because of one's faith. There are works that are *excluded* when it comes to justification by faith (Rom. 4:2), and there are works that are *included* when it comes to faith that justifies (Jam. 2:21-24). Actually, faith is the work in a sense that God requires it of man which is expressed in turning to Jesus. (See John 6:29 and Romans 10:10.) The Ninevites expressed their faith by their works and God was moved to forgive them. It was faith that saved them but faith that saves is faith that submits. Today one must believe and be baptized and God will be moved to save him (Mk. 16:16).

GOD RELENTS OF THE SEVERITY.

God actually *retracted* the *punishment* (3:10b). God relented of the evil. In other words, He withdrew the punishment. This is in keeping with the principle that Jeremiah lays down in Jeremiah 18:5-10. God spoke concerning Nineveh "to destroy it," but they "turned from their evil" and God "relented from the disaster" and did it not. Today God has spoken concerning the punishment that is to come on the wicked (Matt. 25:46; 2 Thess. 1:6-9). But He will withdraw that punishment from all who, like Nineveh, will repent and turn to Jesus for salvation. God not only retracted the punishment, He also *reacted* with *pardon*. Nineveh was pardoned because of God's mercy. Someone has said that grace is "getting what we *do not* deserve" while mercy is "not getting what we *do* deserve." The Ninevites deserved to be destroyed but they did not get what they deserved. Why? Because of God's mercy. Jonah knew that God was "gracious and merciful..." (4:2). It was knowing about the Lord's mercy that caused Jonah to repent of his own rebellion (2:8). The book of Jonah shows us that God is merciful to the *wicked* (1:2; 3:10), to the *wayward* (chs.1-2), and to the *weak* (ch. 4). All men need to know of God's mercy because it is "according to His mercy" that He saves us (Titus 3:5). In Psalms 103 David speaks of how God is abounding in mercy (v.8). He also gives us a picture of God's mercy (v.13). And finally, he talks about the permanency of God's mercy (v.17). It is also interesting that all twenty-six verses of Psalms 136 end with the same phrase: "His mercy endures forever." If the Lord is our Shepherd, then we can say with the psalmist: "Surely goodness and mercy shall follow me all the days of my life and I will dwell in the house of the Lord for ever" (Ps. 23:6). We can be "looking for the mercy of our Lord Jesus Christ unto eternal life" (Jude 1:21). When

Nineveh believed the message, then God bestowed the mercy. And He will do the same for us "for His mercy endures forever."

In chapter three we have seen Jonah *responding* and running *with* God. His *message* to Nineveh caused them to *mourn* over their sins which caused God to extend *mercy* to them. In our next study, chapter four, we will see Jonah *resenting* what God did in chapter three.

DISCUSSION QUESTIONS

LESSON 9

1. What did God see in Nineveh according to Jonah 3:10?

2. Why is it detrimental to our spiritual growth for us to believe that God sees us only when we do wrong?

3. Give examples of those whom the Lord commended for doing good.

4. Prove that repentance is an expression of faith.

5. Describe the difference between works of faith and works of merit.

6. Why is believing called a "work of God" (John 6:29)? When God "saw their works" (3:10a), was their faith included in what God saw? (See Jonah 3:5.)

7. What did God do when He saw their works? Explain God's action in light of Jeremiah 18:5-10.

8. Discuss the difference between grace and mercy.

9. What is unusual about Psalms 136?

10. Give at least one passage from the New Testament that proves we are saved by God's mercy rather than by our own merit.

CHAPTER FOUR

JONAH RESENTING
(Running against God)

I. THE GRIEF (4:1-5). The grief is shown.

A. His Displeasure with God's Conduct (4:1).
  1. The attitude of the prophet (v.1a).
  2. The anger of the prophet (v.1b).

B. His Discernment of God's Character (4:2).
  1. What He had said (v.2).
  2. Why he had fled (v.2).

C. His Disappointment with God's Compassion (4:3-4).
  1. His longing to die (v.3).
  2. His Lord's reply (v.4).

D. His Departure from the Great City (4:5).
  1. Where he went to sit (v.5a).
  2. What he wanted to see (v.5b).

II. THE GOURD (4:6-9). The gourd is gone.

A. The plant is Supplied (4:6).
   1. The reason for the plant (v.6a).
   2. The relief for the prophet (v.6b).

B. The plant is Smitten (4:7-9).
   1. The worm (v.7a).
   2. The withering (v.7b).
   3. The wind (v.8a).
   4. The wish (vv.8b, 9).

III. THE GOODNESS (4:10-11). The goodness is made known.

A. Jehovah's Pity (4:10-11).
   1. What God said to the prophet.
   2. Why God spared the people.

B. Jonah's Problem (4:10-11).
   1. He was concerned about the plant.
   2. He didn't care about the people.

LESSON 10

SCRIPTURE READING
(Jonah 4:1-11)

BUT IT DISPLEASED JONAH EXCEEDINGLY, *and he was angry. 2 And he prayed to the Lord and said, "O Lord, is not this what I said when I was yet in my country? That is why I made haste to flee to Tarshish; for I knew that you are a gracious God and merciful, slow to anger and abounding in steadfast love, and relenting from disaster. 3 Therefore now, O Lord, please take my life from me, for it is better for me to die than to live." 4 And the Lord said, "Do you do well to be angry?"*

⁵ Jonah went out of the city and sat to the east of the city and made a booth for himself there. He sat under it in the shade, till he should see what would become of the city. ⁶ Now the LORD GOD APPOINTED A PLANT *and made it come up over Jonah, that it might be a shade over his head, to save him from his discomfort. So Jonah was exceedingly glad because of the plant. ⁷ But when dawn came up the next day, God appointed a worm that attacked the plant, so that it withered.*

⁸ When the sun rose, God appointed a scorching east wind, and the sun beat down on the head of Jonah so that he was faint. And he asked that he might die and said, "It is better for me to die than to live." ⁹ But God said to Jonah, "Do you do well to be angry for the plant?" And he said, "Yes, I do well to be angry, angry enough to die." ¹⁰ And the LORD SAID, "YOU PITY THE PLANT, FOR WHICH YOU DID NOT LABOR, NOR DID YOU MAKE IT GROW, WHICH CAME INTO BEING IN A NIGHT AND PERISHED IN A NIGHT. *¹¹ And should not I pity Nineveh, that great city, in which there are more than 120,000 persons who do not know their right hand from their left, and also much cattle?"* (ESV)

LESSON 10

JONAH RESENTING
(Running against God)
Jonah 4:1-11

IN THIS TENTH AND FINAL lesson from the book of Jonah, we are going to study the entire fourth chapter in this one lesson. In chapter one, we saw Jonah *rebelling* and running *from* God. In chapter two, we saw Jonah *repenting* and running *to* God. In chapter three, we saw Jonah *responding* and running *with* God. And here in chapter four we're going to see him *resenting* and running *against* God. We've learned about the Lord's presence in chapter one, His pardon in chapter two, and His power in chapter three. Now we'll study about His passion. In this study we will notice the grief, the gourd, the goodness.

THE GRIEF (4:1-5).
(The grief is shown)

First we observe Jonah's *displeasure* with God's

conduct (4:1). The attitude of the prophet is almost unbelievable. The verse says, "But it displeased Jonah exceedingly." He was displeased that God spared Nineveh. The degree of his anger is emphasized by the word *very*. He was not simply angry, he was very angry. He was actually grieved because of God's goodness. He was mad because of God's mercy. Most preachers are displeased when people do not respond favorably, but Jonah was displeased because Nineveh did! He had the same spirit that the elder brother had who was angry that his younger brother had been forgiven (Lk. 15:25-28). Second, let us observe his *discernment* of God's *character* (4:2). Jonah had a good insight into the character of God. This we see in *what he had said*. He also tells us *why he had fled*. The reason that he fled to Tarshish in the first place is because of what he knew about the character of God. He knew that God would spare the Ninevites if they repented, and he didn't want them spared. He wanted them destroyed. He was a pitiless preacher—a powerful patriot but a pitiless preacher (2 Kings 14:25). The book of Jonah deals with a *wicked city* and a *lack of pity*. Third, observe his *disappointment* with God's *compassion* (4:3-4). In verse three, he is so disappointed with God's compassion for Nineveh that he *longs to die*. At least, that is what he says he wants. Whether or not he really meant it is questionable. But there is no question concerning his disappointment. He was really unhappy because they were spared. Are we ever disappointed when one of our enemies, or one who has wronged us, repents and is forgiven by God? When he longs to die, let us see *the Lord's reply* (4:4). It seems that He wanted Jonah to think about his attitude and so He asked, "Is it right for you to be angry?" This is a good question for us to ask ourselves anytime we get angry. Anger is not sinful if we are angry about the right things and if the anger doesn't cause us to sin (Ps. 7:11; Mk. 3:5; Matt. 5:22; Eph. 4:26). Jonah's anger was wrong because he was not angry for the right reason; therefore, his anger caused him to act like a spoiled child. Anger is just one letter short of the word *danger*. And any time there is anger we are mighty close to danger. The thing that might help us in these situations is to remember the question that God asked Jonah, "Is it right for me to be angry?" Next we observe his *departure* from the *city* (4:5). Jonah went out to sit on the east side of the city. He wanted to see what would become of the city. He was seemingly still hoping that God would somehow destroy it. There are some sins and weaknesses that are really hard to overcome. Jonah's sin of prejudice falls into that category. And all of us have certain sins that "easily ensnares us" (Heb. 12:1).

THE GOURD PLANT (4:6-9).
(The gourd is gone)

In His effort to help Jonah we see that a gourd plant is s*upplied* (4:6). The reason for the plant is given in verse six. It was to *relieve the prophet*. Note: Some older translations such as the KJV, ASV, and Young's Literal Translation say "gourd," but the modern versions say "plant." Yet none seem to know what kind of "plant" it was. So I just call it a "gourd plant." The text says that the plant was prepared to deliver him from his grief. The plant was actually prepared in order to help Jonah understand why God had spared the city. Observe that Jonah was "very grateful" for the plant. He was exceedingly mad because Nineveh repented (4: l), but very grateful for a plant that served as a shade for himself. But after the plant is supplied, it is then s*mitten* (4:7-9). In these verses we have the *worm, withering, wind,* and *wish*. God prepared a worm which smote the plant and it withered, so Jonah's shade was gone. Then God prepared an east wind which, along with the heat of the sun, caused Jonah to have a sun-stroke. And he wished again to die. Remember, God's discipline is not always pleasant (Heb. 12:5-12). In fact, when God asked him again, "Is it right for you to be angry about the plant?" He answered by saying in essence, "Yes, I do well to be angry. I'm so mad I could die!" Not only had God spared the wicked Ninevites but now Jonah's gourd plant was gone!

THE GOODNESS (4:10- 11).
(The goodness is made known)

Observe Jehovah's *pity*. If we notice what God *said to the prophet*, we will find out why God *spared the people*. He spared them because of His goodness and pity on them. And if Jonah cared for a plant that he had neither planted nor cultivated, because of its usefulness to him, shouldn't God be concerned about a great city that He had caused to be brought into existence and had sustained its inhabitants by giving them "life, breath, and all things" (Acts17:25b)? What was Jonah's problem? *He cared more about plants than he did about people.* He did not even care for the innocent ones who may have not yet reached the age of accountability. Many of us today are greatly concerned about things that directly affect our comforts (air-conditioning, padded pews, nice buildings, etc.), but are we really concerned at all about the souls of dying people who will go into eternity unprepared to meet God. Let us learn the lesson that Jonah evidently learned: God is far more concerned about *souls* than He is about *things.* Let us remember that the book of Jonah emphasizes the goodness of God toward all men. He is "a gracious and merciful God, slow to anger, and abundant in loving kindness" (4:2).

In this final lesson from Jonah, we have noticed how the *grief* brought about the *gourd* which helped Jonah understand God's *goodness.* We hope that Jonah learned his lesson. But even if he did not learn, he left us an example by which we can profit.

DISCUSSION QUESTIONS

LESSON 10

1. One of the definitions that Webster gives for passion is "strong love and affection." How is the Lord's passion demonstrated in chapter four?

2. What was Jonah's reaction to the sparing of Nineveh? What New Testament character manifested that same spirit?

3. How do we know that Jonah had a good insight into the character of God? Why did Jonah refuse to go to Nineveh in the first place?

4. Is all anger sin? Did Jonah sin through anger? Support your answers.

5. God asked Jonah: "Is it right for you to be angry?" How can this question help us today?

6. Why did God prepare the plant for Jonah and what was Jonah's reaction?

7. Why did God destroy the plant and what was Jonah's reaction?

8. How did God use the plant to teach Jonah a much needed lesson?

9. What do we need to learn about *things and people* from the fourth chapter of Jonah?

10. One of the main lessons we need to learn and remember about God in the book of Jonah is clearly stated here in chapter four. What is it?

Wayne Dunaway

Revised October 2017

www.ingramcontent.com/pod-product-compliance
Lightning Source LLC
Chambersburg PA
CBHW070523030426
42337CB00016B/2086